GLORY

PHOTOGRAPHS BY

ROBERT D'ALESSANDRO

★

ELEPHANT PUBLISHING CORPORATION

NEW YORK CITY

To my father

Printed in the United States of America
Library of Congress Catalog Card Number: 74–79168
ISBN 0–914654–00–4

Brooklyn, New York, 1972

Brooklyn, New York, 1970

Long Island, New York, 1970

Jersey City, New Jersey, 1971

The Jersey Meadows, New Jersey, 1972

Brooklyn, New York, 1971

Cliffside, New Jersey, 1971

Myrtle Avenue, Brooklyn, New York, 1972

Fourteenth Street, New York City, 1970

Long Island City, New York, 1971

North Bergen, New Jersey, 1971

Albuquerque, New Mexico, 1970

Sunrise Highway, Long Island, New York, 1972

Pennsylvania Turnpike, 1971

New Orleans, Louisiana, 1971

Sixth Avenue, New York City, 1969

New York City, 1972

Broadway, New York City, 1970

Long Island, New York, 1972

New York City, 1972

Jersey City, New Jersey, 1971

Fourteenth Street, New York City, 1971

Brooklyn, New York, 1970

Atlantic Avenue, Brooklyn, New York, 1971

New York City, 1970

Westhampton Beach, New York, July 4th 1970

Memphis, Tennessee, 1971

Buffalo, New York, 1971

Bedford-Stuyvesant, Brooklyn, New York, 1971

Wheeling, West Virginia, 1970

Bedford–Stuyvesant, Brooklyn, New York, 1971

Jersey City, New Jersey, 1971

Islip, New York, Memorial Day 1970

Hoboken, New Jersey, 1969

Brooklyn, New York, 1970

Flushing, New York, 1972

Eastport, New York, 1969

Albuquerque, New Mexico, 1973

Madison, New Jersey, 1972

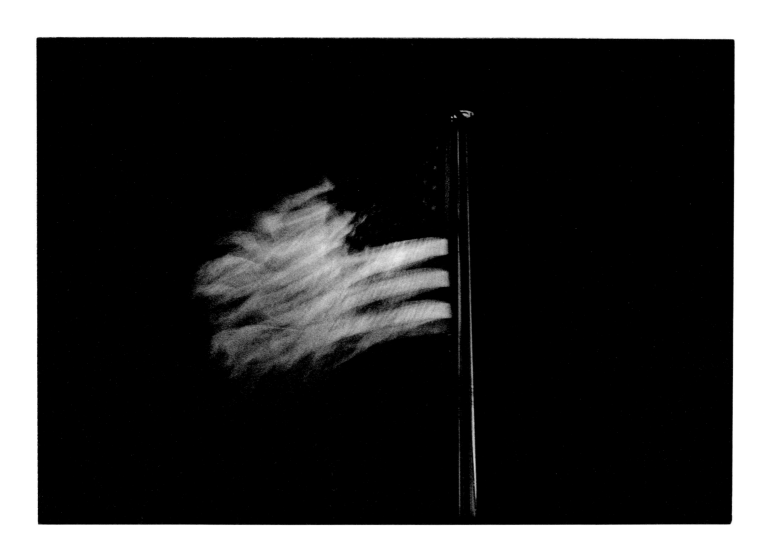

Designed by Marvin Hoshino
Produced by Sara D'Alessandro

My thanks to Fanny Cusumanno,
Marvin Hoshino, Charles Pratt, Richard Westley,
and to William L. Broecker.

R. D.